Fundamen-talisman

Resurrecting the
Fundamentals of Relationship
from the
Fundamentalism of Religion

By Duann Kier

ISBN-10: 1461115876
ISBN-13: 978-1461115878

Dedication

to all who face their fear and find freedom

Acknowledgments

Grateful gratitude is given to

my friend Libby Freeland, and her husband Bill, for giving me a heavenly place to write

my friend (and editor), Joyce Counihan, for being involved in this process from the very beginning and always encouraging me onward and upward

Table of Contents

Preface

If you are a Christian fundamentalist and your beliefs are working for you because you know beyond a shadow of a doubt that they are right and real, this book is probably *not* for you. If you are a Christian fundamentalist and are beginning to question some of the beliefs you've been taught along the way, this book *may* be for you. If you are—or once were—a Christian fundamentalist and your beliefs just aren't working for you anymore, this book is *definitely* for you.

Hello. My name is Duann and I am a former fundamentalist.

Does that statement make you feel somewhat uncomfortable? Are you wondering whether you should just put this book down and walk away? Are you feeling concerned for me and where I might be spending eternity? Do you feel a burden on your heart to witness to me? Are you uneasy that God may hold you accountable for my soul if you don't witness to me? Are you afraid to contemplate any religions or spiritual principles different from your own because of God's potential judgment and wrath?

Fear not! According to the Gospel of John in the New Testament of the Bible, Jesus says "ye shall know the truth, and the truth shall make you free" (Chapter 8, Verse 32, KJV). So, let's begin with your trying to give some truthful answers to some rather soul-searching questions:

- Would you be a Christian *if* there were no heaven or hell?

- Is the fear of hell the *main* reason you are a Christian?

- Do you sometimes wonder whether you are *really* saved from hell?

- Do you *really* have the peace that passes all understanding?

- Do you find no matter how hard you try, you just can't seem to be the person that you want to be? The person that you know *God* wants you to be?

- Do you *truly* feel loved and cherished by your creator?

These are not comfortable questions to ask oneself, and you may have already put the book down by now. But if you haven't done that yet, I encourage you to stay with me to its end. It promises to be a real page-turner for you.

Fundamen-talisman

Introduction

So how did you end up here? What's a nice girl, or guy, like you from a Christian fundamentalist background doing in a place like this? And where is all of this going?

Well, for starters, you probably began this journey by becoming a born again Christian sometime in your life. It could have been a natural, normal process of growing up in your specific family. It could have been a particularly dark time in your life and the message of Jesus brought you light and hope. It could have been your life was in absolute shambles and you begged for God to intervene and give you direction. It could have been any number of other reasons as well, but in summary, you probably wanted a direct, personal relationship with your creator.

You were probably told in some form or fashion that the "instruction manual" for this relationship could be found in the Bible—the literal, inerrant, divine, final, and only word, of the one and only true God, and his one and only begotten son, your personal Lord and Savior Jesus Christ.

What a joyous and magical day it was when you became a Christian! You were no longer alone. You had joined a big and beautiful and loving family of all the Christians in the world and throughout all of history. You felt like all of the world's burdens had been magically lifted off your shoulders and you just wanted to shout out from the roof tops that life is good because God is good!

You actually enjoyed going to church—being with your brothers and sisters, studying God's word, hungering and thirsting after righteousness sake. It was a brand-spanking new, bright and beautiful world.

Then something began to change. You're not exactly sure when it began or how it came about, but somehow it became less and less about being part of God's loving family and it became more and more about saving yourself and others from hell. What happened? Did you really begin to feel that God expected you to make sure each and every person on the planet heard about his love and how he had sacrificed his own son for them? Did the sense of responsibility overwhelm you? Did you feel uncomfortable trying to save someone else's soul when you sometimes actually doubted your *own* salvation from the fires of hell? Did you maybe begin to wonder just a little bit about why you were supposed to *fear* a loving God and why he had to have someone to *punish* for your being so evil? And did you put the doubts out of your mind over and over again by rationalizing that God had to be just; that is, *because* God is just, he must see that justice is done? Did you then try to rationalize the love of God because he was willing to send his one and only begotten son to be your substitute for his just punishment?

I did.

I confess I began this whole process just wanting to be part of a big loving family. I wanted to belong somewhere. I wanted to feel safe and secure and protected and happy. I already felt pretty much worthless for a multitude of reasons, so knowing that I was probably on my way to hell wasn't much of a stretch for me. When I "got saved" in my teenage years, I just wanted to get on, with going on, to heaven. It's just that I never quite felt like I was going to make it. I wanted to, but I knew I still had these really, really sinful thoughts and feelings that Christians probably shouldn't have. Then I'd rededicate my life—even got baptized a second time—to try to wipe my slate clean all over and over and over again. If I was a Christian, shouldn't I be feeling a sense of freedom from my burdens as opposed to feeling more burdened than I had ever felt in my entire life? I knew God was continually watching me and finding me lacking as one of his children. I began to believe I was even more worthless than I had originally thought.

So, you already know how the psychology works. The more worthless you feel, the more you have to compensate for it. You become increasingly paranoid that others will realize that you aren't the gen-u-ine article. You try harder and harder and harder to become the gen-u-ine article, or at least to look like you are. You follow all the rules and all the regulations and become more and more uptight about your failures, even if they are known only to you. You become more and more legalistic and judgmental of yourself and, of course, others. You begin to resent *them*. Why aren't *they* following all the rules and regulations? Why aren't *they* seeing all the errors of *their* ways? Why aren't *they* trying as hard as I am?

And then something strange begins to happen. It's even stranger than strange. *You begin to feel a little bit better than everyone else because—at least—you are trying!* The focus begins to change, from trying so hard to patting yourself on the back for trying at all. I mean, look at all of those other people out there who aren't even trying to be godly! Just by the process of elimination, you should make it through those pearly gates onto the golden streets of heaven, right?

A false sense of compassion begins to develop inside of you for those others that you're supposed to be loving. Why, bless their hearts! They just aren't going to be able to make it now, are they? You'll do what you can to help, but they could choose to get right with God just the way you did, couldn't they? And if they haven't heard about Jesus, there should be something deep down inside their heart of hearts telling them to look for him. It did yours, right?

But this is where it all begins to fall apart. There was definitely something inside of you looking for something when you found Jesus. You thought at the time that you had found *it*, but now you're not so sure. There just seems to be so very many questions still haunting you. It frightens you even to think about asking them because it might mean the whole thing really does fall apart. Where would that leave you? Isn't it all you have left?

Well, for all intents and purposes, what's left might be even better than what you've got. Let's dare to take the challenge of asking some of those threatening questions and fundamentally see what's left. I know it's scary. It certainly was for me. But God helped me face my fears and find freedom from them. I have faith that he can, and will, do the same for you, too. And I don't believe it will put you back on that same road straight for hell all over again.

Chapter One

Is the Bible the *Literal* Word of God?

If you're still a Christian fundamentalist, your automatic answer to the question above may very be, "Well yes, of course it is!"

May I ask you another question? Are you already feeling just a little bit defensive about my even asking the question? If so, please refer back to what I said in the preface:

> *If you are a Christian fundamentalist and your beliefs are working for you because you know beyond a shadow of a doubt that they are right and real, this book is probably **not** for you.*

You can stop reading this book now and put it down. You never ever have to have anything else to do with it again for as long as you live. But if you do want to continue reading, let's look at the word "literal."

Literal is the opposite of figurative or metaphorical; that is, symbolic or representative of something deeper than what is being described. Metaphorical or symbolic language is one of the teaching techniques that Jesus used when he told parables. Could it be that the Bible quite frequently uses this same technique? For example, is the following passage from the Bible meant to be taken literally?

> *Jesus answered and said unto him, Verily, verily, I say unto thee, except a man be **born again**, he cannot see the kingdom of God (John 3:3, KJV).*

You can see the problem with a literal interpretation of this passage. To *literally* be "born again" means that we would have to go back into our mother's womb so she can give birth to us again. Actually, as much weight as being "born again" has been given in evangelical Christianity, this is the only place where it appears in the Bible.

We could look at examples of this throughout the whole Bible or just the New Testament or even just the Gospels. But let's narrow it down even further to looking at some examples from just the words of Jesus as recorded in the other three Gospels.

> *For all the prophets and the law prophesied until **John**. And if ye will receive it, this **is Elias**, which was for to come (Matthew 11:12-14, KJV).*

Literally interpreted, we should take this to mean that John the Baptist was Elias (Greek for Elijah), one of the Old Testament prophets. Are we talking about reincarnation here? Or, how about this one?

> *And as they did eat, Jesus took bread, and blessed, and brake it, and gave to them, and said, **Take, eat: this is my body** (Mark 14:22, KJV).*

I doubt we want to interpret this as Jesus promoting cannibalism, especially of himself. And then there's this troubling passage as well.

> *If any man come to me, and **hate** not his father, and mother, and wife, and children,*

and brethren, and sisters, yea, and his own life also, he cannot be my disciple (Luke 14:26, KJV).

I personally choose to believe that loving one's father, mother, spouse and siblings does not disqualify one from being a disciple of Jesus.

Any idea where you learned that the Bible is the *literal* word of God? To the best of my knowledge, it's nowhere in the Bible. You might be saying to yourself by now, though, "Well, I didn't mean that every single word in the Bible is the literal word of God." Even at the risk of alienating you at this point, I feel the need to point out that you can't have it both ways. If you do have it both ways, you have to decide which words are the literal words of God and which words aren't. Then you have to decide who gets to make those decisions.

You might assume that a really committed Christian will be able to tell the difference, but Christians have been arguing over the interpretation of biblical passages probably ever since there have been biblical passages. Does that mean that they aren't committed Christians?

Even committed Christians believe that three wise men came to visit Jesus when he was just a baby lying in a manger, but nowhere in the Bible does it say that this is the case. If I just got a raised eyebrow from you, please feel free to double-check me on this (which I'm sure you will).

Traditionally, most Christians believe that three kings from the Orient followed a star to find and honor the newborn infant Jesus in his manger in a stable in Bethlehem. Matthew is the only gospel in the Bible that reports this particular event, but the story told there is quite different from the one with which most of us are familiar.

In the second chapter of Matthew, it states that "there came wise men from the east to Jerusalem." There is no mention of how many wise men or that they were kings or that they were specifically from the Orient or eastern Asia. Matthew shares that the men have seen a star in the east, and that the star later goes before them, but he also tells us that it is actually Herod who "sent them to Bethlehem." Further on he expresses that "when they were come into the house, they saw the young child with Mary his mother, and fell down, and worshipped him." Here we have a house and a young child. There is no mention of a manger or a stable or of Jesus being a newborn infant. Indications are this visit happened much later than when we have come to assume.

What I'm trying to point out here is that even committed Christians who believe the Bible is the *literal* word of God may be making assumptions about what is *literally* in the Bible.

May I suggest that you really don't believe that the Bible is the *literal* word of God? You probably understand that many of its passages are metaphorical or symbolic. But maybe you believe the Bible is the *inerrant* word of God.

Chapter Two

Is the Bible the *Inerrant* Word of God?

After asking whether the Bible is the *literal* word of God, you may now be feeling a little uncomfortable asking if it is the *inerrant* word of God.

As I have already said, you can put this book down right now and never ever have anything else to do with it. But, then again, if you do want to keep reading, let's look at what the word "inerrant" means.

When something is inerrant, it is free from error; that is, free from mistakes or inaccuracies. Unfortunately, the Bible doesn't seem to be free of these. Let's begin at the beginning with a passage in the Bible describing the creation of man.

And God made the beast of the earth after his kind, and cattle after their kind, and every thing that creepeth upon the earth after his kind: and God saw that it was good. And God said, Let us make man in our image, after our likeness: and let them have dominion over the fish of the sea, and over the fowl of the air, and over the cattle, and over all the earth, and over every creeping thing that creepeth upon the earth (Genesis 1:25-26, KJV).

As you can see from this passage, God made animals first, and then he created man and gave him dominion over them. But in the very next chapter, we get a different story.

And the LORD God said, It is not good that the man should be alone; I will make him an help meet for him. And out of the ground the LORD God formed every beast of the field, and every fowl of the air; and brought them unto Adam to see what he would call them: and whatsoever Adam called every living creature, that was the name thereof (Genesis 2:18-19, KJV).

In this passage, God made man first and then he created the animals because it was not good for man to be alone.

Of course, it may not make any difference to your faith which came first—man or animals. But it stills begs the question of whether the Bible is the *inerrant* word of God. A little later in the biblical story we find another discrepancy.

> *Of every clean beast thou shalt take to thee by* **sevens***, the male and his female: and of beasts that are not clean by* **two***, the male and his female. Of fowls also of the air by* **sevens***, the male and the female (Genesis 7:2, KJV).*

> *Of clean beasts, and of beasts that are not clean, and of fowls, and of every thing that creepeth upon the earth, There went in* **two** *and* **two** *unto Noah into the ark, the male and the female, as God had commanded Noah (Genesis 7:8, KJV).*

How many animals was Noah told to take? Even if you try to explain away this discrepancy by saying "two and two" refers to the male and female of each animal, you still aren't going to come up with the number seven.

And how did Saul, the first king of the united kingdom of Israel, die? Was it suicide?

And the battle went sore against Saul, and the archers hit him; and he was sore wounded of the archers. Then said Saul unto his armourbearer, Draw thy sword, and thrust me through therewith; lest these uncircumcised come and thrust me through, and abuse me. But his armourbearer would not; for he was sore afraid. Therefore Saul took a sword, and fell upon it (1 Samuel 31:3-4, KJV).

Or was he slain by the Philistines?

And David went and took the bones of Saul and the bones of Jonathan his son from the men of Jabesh-gilead, which had stolen them from the street of Beth-shan, where the Philistines had hanged them, when the Philistines had slain Saul in Gilboa (2 Samuel 21:12, KJV).

The Philistines sorely wounded Saul, but he committed suicide before they had a chance to slay him. I guess you could argue that it was the Philistines bearing down on him that caused him to commit suicide, but they still were not the actual cause of death. Even though the bottom line is that Saul died in the battle with the Philistines, it is still two different versions of the same story.

A more problematic issue may be in regards to who told King David to number Israel.

> *And again the anger of the LORD was kindled against Israel, and he moved David against them to say, Go, number Israel and Judah (2 Samuel 24:1, KJV).*

> *And Satan stood up against Israel, and provoked David to number Israel (1 Chronicles 21:1, KJV).*

This is a rather dramatic example of how much difference can be found in the same story. It gets even more complicated when two diametrically opposed positions are purported, such as how we should view our enemies.

> *The righteous shall rejoice when he seeth the vengeance: he shall wash his feet in the blood of the wicked (Psalm 58:10, KJV).*

> *Rejoice not when thine enemy falleth, and let not thine heart be glad when he stumbleth (Proverbs 24:17, KJV)*

Again, this probably doesn't directly affect your own personal faith, yet there are multiple examples where the biblical text is found not to be infallible or absolute. In fact, there are so many of these instances in the New Testament gospels that there have been concerted efforts to compare them side by side in an attempt to place the events in some sort of explicable order. Rather than adding to the case for inerrancy, these attempts seem to shine a more glaring light on the disparities.

For example, after Jesus' birth in Bethlehem, one account tells us that Joseph is warned in a dream to flee to Egypt.

> *And when they were departed, behold, the angel of the Lord appeareth to Joseph in a dream, saying, Arise, and take the young child and his mother, and flee into Egypt, and be thou there until I bring thee word: for Herod will seek the young child to destroy him (Matthew 2:13, KJV).*

In another account, we are told the family goes to Jerusalem rather than Egypt. In fact, Egypt is never even mentioned.

And when the days of her purification according to the law of Moses were accomplished, they brought him to Jerusalem, to present him to the Lord. . . .And when they had performed all things according to the law of the Lord, they returned into Galilee, to their own city Nazareth (Luke 2:22, 39, KJV).

We also have different versions of what went on between Jesus and Pilate. In one version, Jesus utters not a word.

Then said Pilate unto him, Hearest thou not how many things they witness against thee? And he answered him to never a word; insomuch that the governor marvelled greatly (Matthew 27:13-14, KJV).

In another version, Jesus seems to preach a whole philosophical sermon.

Pilate answered, Am I a Jew? Thine own nation and the chief priests have delivered thee unto me: what hast thou done? Jesus answered, My kingdom is not of this world: if my kingdom were of this world, then would my servants fight, that I should not be delivered to the Jews: but now is my kingdom not from hence.

Pilate therefore said unto him, Art thou a king then? Jesus answered, Thou sayest that I am a king. To this end was I born, and for this cause came I into the world, that I should bear witness unto the truth. Every one that is of the truth heareth my voice (John 18:35-37, KJV).

There also seem to be inconsistencies about the last words of Jesus on the cross.

*And when Jesus had cried with a loud voice, he said, **Father, into thy hands I commend my spirit**: and having said thus, he gave up the ghost (Luke 23:46, KJV).*

*When Jesus therefore had received the vinegar, he said, **It is finished**: and he bowed his head, and gave up the ghost (John 19:30, KJV).*

There are even different accounts regarding when and where Jesus ascended into heaven.

Afterward he appeared unto the eleven as they sat at meat, and upbraided them with their unbelief and hardness of heart, because they believed not them which had seen him after he was risen. . . .So then after the Lord had spoken unto them, he was received up into heaven, and sat on the right hand of God (Mark 16:14, 19, KJV).

And he led them out as far as to Bethany, and he lifted up his hands, and blessed them. And it came to pass, while he blessed them, he was parted from them, and carried up into heaven (Luke 24:50-51, KJV).

And when he had spoken these things, while they beheld, he was taken up; and a cloud received him out of their sight. . . .Then returned they unto Jerusalem from the mount called Olivet, which is from Jerusalem a sabbath day's journey (Acts 1:9, 12, KJV).

You've probably already noticed many of the contradictions in the Bible and don't actually believe in its *inerrancy.* You don't have to believe in that or its literalism to still believe it is the word of God because you believe it is *divinely inspired.*

Chapter Three

Is the Bible the *Divinely Inspired* Word of God?

Well, since you've made it this far in the book without throwing it away, my guess is you'll probably make it through this chapter as well. It probably isn't because you'll agree with everything you read here—or that you've agreed with everything you've already read—but you may have become a little bit more comfortable asking some of the questions we're asking.

So what does "divinely inspired" mean? When something is deemed *divine*, it is more often than not perceived as coming from God. And *inspiration* usually means some sort of stirring or urging. So when something is referred to as being divinely inspired, we can surmise it alludes to a stirring or urging from God.

Regrettably, if the Bible is indeed divinely inspired, God seems to be a proponent of some ideas that most of us would find personally objectionable.

For instance, according to many biblical passages, God has absolutely no qualms about slaughtering innocent women and children or allowing them to be exploited by perfect strangers.

Now therefore kill every male among the little ones, and kill every woman that hath known man by lying with him. But all the women children, that have not known a man by lying with him, keep alive for yourselves (Numbers 31:17-18, KJV).

When thou goest forth to war against thine enemies, and the LORD thy God hath delivered them into thine hands, and thou hast taken them captive, And seest among the captives a beautiful woman, and hast a desire unto her, that thou wouldest have her to thy wife Then thou shalt bring her home to thine house (Deuteronomy 21:10-12, KJV).

Their children also shall be dashed to pieces before their eyes; their houses shall be spoiled, and their wives ravished. Behold, I will stir up the Medes against them, which shall not regard silver; and as for gold, they shall not delight in it. Their bows also shall dash the young men to pieces; and they shall have no pity on the fruit of the womb; their eyes shall not spare children (Isaiah 13:16-18, KJV).

Not a very pretty picture, is it?

Then there are also passages which indicate that God actually sets up certain people or groups to be destroyed.

For it was of the LORD to harden their hearts, that they should come against Israel in battle, that he might destroy them utterly, and that they might have no favour, but that he might destroy them, as the LORD commanded Moses (Joshua 11:20, KJV).

And if the prophet be deceived when he hath spoken a thing, I the LORD have deceived that prophet, and I will stretch out my hand upon him, and will destroy him from the midst of my people Israel (Ezekiel 14:9, KJV).

Even if we could still hold that the Bible is divinely inspired, we don't really seem to feel any great burden to follow its admonitions in these particular instances.

> *Ye shall keep my statutes. Thou shalt not let thy cattle gender with a diverse kind: thou shalt not sow thy field with mingled seed: neither shall a garment mingled of linen and woollen come upon thee (Leviticus 19:19, KJV).*

> *Ye have heard that it hath been said, An eye for an eye, and a tooth for a tooth: But I say unto you, that ye resist not evil: but whosoever shall smite thee on thy right cheek, turn to him the other also. And if any man will sue thee at the law, and take away thy coat, let him have thy cloak also (Matthew 5:38-40, KJV).*

> *And call no man your father upon the earth: for one is your Father, which is in heaven (Matthew 23:9, KJV).*

> *Doth not even nature itself teach you, that, if a man have long hair, it is a shame unto him? (1 Corinthians 11:14, KJV).*

Do we not wear clothes that are a blend of linen and wool? Do we not protect ourselves from someone who has just hit us? Do we not call our father, "Father"? Do we not assume that Jesus had long hair?

And we choose to completely ignore the incongruity of this particular passage.

> *Verily I say unto you, There be some standing here, which shall not taste of death, till they see the Son of man coming in his kingdom (Matthew 16:28, KJV).*

What seems particularly disturbing about divine inspiration is how easily we can ignore it when it doesn't suit our purposes and how easily we can claim it when it supports our bigotry and intolerance toward those who are different from us (i.e., supporting slavery in Leviticus 25:45 and condemning same sex relationships while overlooking the gang rape of women in Genesis 19).

This selective texting has actually led to justifiable mass murder. Here are a couple of scriptural justifications used during a period of our history known as the "burning times."

> *Thou shalt not suffer a witch to live (Exodus 22:18, KJV).*

There shall not be found among you any one that maketh his son or his daughter to pass through the fire, or that useth divination, or an observer of times, or an enchanter, or a witch (Deuteronomy 18:10, KJV).

This is particularly interesting when one considers that the chosen people of God made decisions and foretold the future by

- casting lots (i.e., to divide the land of Canaan in Numbers 26:55 and to choose Matthias as an apostle to replace Judas in Acts 1:26)

- getting messages in dreams (i.e., Jacob's son Joseph in Genesis 41:25, Daniel in Daniel 4:19 and Mary's husband Joseph in Matthew 1 & 2)

- receiving visitations by angels (i.e., stopping Abraham from killing his son Isaac in Genesis 22:11 and telling Mary in Luke 1:26 that she would give birth)

- utilizing the breastplate of judgment, known as the Urim and Thummin (Exodus 28:30), and

- consulting seers:

Beforetime in Israel, when a man went to inquire of God, thus he spake, Come, and let us go to the seer: for he that is now called a Prophet was beforetime called a Seer (I Samuel 9:9, KJV).

This particular chapter in the book may have ended up being the most difficult one for you so far. It may now feel like trash for the garbage since it's shown light on things you'd rather leave in the dark. But, believe or not, this is actually where I'm going to point out to you that the Bible does indeed have some incredibly amazing truths in it. To find them, it's necessary to continue with asking our next question. Is the Bible the *only* word of God?

Chapter Four

Is the Bible the

Only Word of God?

You are probably quite familiar with the biblical story as presented in the Old Testament. It begins with Adam and Eve and goes through Noah and the flood and finally comes down to a Hebrew by the name of Abraham who is originally from Sumeria. His son, Isaac, fathers a son named Jacob who later becomes known as Israel. Israel then has twelve sons who become known as the twelve tribes of Israel, or the Israelites. One of these twelve sons, Joseph, ends up in a leadership position in Egypt and brings his father and brothers there to live with him during a time of famine.

Much later in the story we find that there is a pharaoh in Egypt who doesn't remember Joseph and who is oppressing the Israelites. This is where Moses comes in. He frees the children of Israel and receives God's law on a mountain in the wilderness. Over a period of time, the Israelites invade and conquer the land of Canaan and divide it among their twelve tribes. Different leaders known as judges, surface here and there, but finally the tribes become a united kingdom ruled successively by three kings.

The first of these kings is Saul, followed by David, and then David's son, Solomon. Upon Solomon's death, the united kingdom splits into two—Israel in the north and Judah in the south. Each kingdom wars with the other and has its own history of kings and prophets until the northern kingdom of Israel is conquered and carried away by the Assyrians. When the Assyrians are conquered by the Babylonians, the southern kingdom of Judah also falls to the Babylonians, including the destruction of the temple in Jerusalem.

When Cyrus the Great of Persia conquers the Babylonians, he issues a decree allowing all peoples exiled in Babylon to resettle their homelands and restore their houses of worship. The Jews begin returning to Jerusalem and they rebuild the temple under the leadership of Zerubbabel. Then they rebuild the walls of Jerusalem under the leadership of Nehemiah, who also begins a movement for religious revitalization. It is during this time that the Jewish priest and scribe, Ezra, comes to Jerusalem and gathers all the people together for the "reading of the book of the law of Moses" (Nehemiah 8:1, KJV).

It is generally accepted by most biblical scholars that it is probably during this period of the Babylonian exile that many of the books of the Hebrew Scriptures were brought together, especially the first five books of the Bible known as the Pentateuch. These are the books of Genesis, Exodus, Leviticus, Numbers and Deuteronomy.

The Babylonians had their own writings, too, of course. One of them, the *Enuma Elish*, is their story of creation that probably came down to them from ancient Sumeria. In it we are told the order in which creation came into being. First we have energy or light and the forming of the planet. Then the land is divided from the water and there is grass and herbs and fruit. Created next are day and night, along with the seasons, followed by fish, birds, creeping things and beasts of the earth. The finale of creation is man, followed by woman.

Sound familiar?

There's also a story called *The Epic of Gilgamesh*. Part of it relates that mankind had grown too large and noisy and that the gods decided to let all of creation be destroyed in a flood. One man, Ut-Napishtim, was told to build a wooden ark sealed with pitch that would have many rooms and at least one door and a window. When the time came, he and some others, along with specimens of all the creatures on the earth, entered the ark. The rains came and even the mountains were covered with water, but finally the ark came to rest on a mountain in the Middle East. Birds were sent out at different times to see if they could find dry land. The first two returned to the ark because they had nowhere to land, but the third one did not. Everyone leaves the ark and they offer an animal sacrifice that the gods can smell. The gods feel remorse for what has happened upon the earth.

Uncanny, isn't it? Even some of the Babylonian *Code of Hammurabi* will sound familiar to you. For example, number 100 states: "If a man put out the eye of another man, his eye shall be put out." Compare this to Exodus 21:24, KJV: "Eye for eye, tooth for tooth, hand for hand, foot for foot."

Even though there seems to be a general consensus that many of the Hebrew Scriptures were brought together during the Babylonian exile, it's not completely clear how that process took place. Today the Hebrew canon known as the *Tanakh* includes 24 books divided into three parts: the Torah (Law or Pentateuch), the Prophets, and the Writings.

There were many books commonly circulated and accepted as being true at the time that were not included in the original collection of these texts. They are frequently referred to today as the Old Testament *Apocrypha*. Some of these may have included:

- First Baruch
- Ecclesiasticus
- First & Second Esdras
- Additions to the Book of Esther
- Epistle of Jeremiah
- Book of Judith
- First & Second Book of Maccabees
- Prayer of Azariah and the Song of the Three Young Men
- Prayer of Manasseh
- Story of Bel and the Dragon
- Story of Susanna

- Book of Tobit
- Wisdom of Solomon

There were also books not included in the original set that have come to be called the *Pseudepigrapha*. These were texts allegedly written by authors who were falsely claiming to be someone important. Some of the following may have been included in that list:

- Assumption of Moses
- Second & Third Baruch
- First & Second Enoch
- Book of Jubilees
- Letter of Aristeas
- Life of Adam and Eve
- Third & Fourth Maccabees
- Martyrdom and Ascension of Isaiah
- Psalms of Solomon
- Sibylline Oracles
- Testaments of the Twelve Patriarchs

After the Persians conquered the Babylonians and many of the Jews had returned to their homeland, a new world power conquered the Persians. They were known as the Medes or the Greeks, and the New Testament story begins after they have been conquered by the Romans.

When Jesus is born, the Jews are becoming more rebellious against Roman occupation. They are looking for the coming of their Messiah to save them by overthrowing the Roman Empire and setting up God's kingdom on earth in Jerusalem. The story told in the second testament is about the life of Jesus, his followers and the events after his crucifixion.

By this time, the Hebrew Scriptures had been translated into the Greek language, and this version is known as the *Septuagint* (Greek for the number 70, approximating the number of translators thought to have worked on the project). In the process, the translators edited many of the books that had been included in the original collection and also chose to include many of the apocryphal books that originally had been left out.

Somewhere along the way, the finalization of the Hebrew canon rejected the *Septuagint*, perhaps at a Council of Jamnia sometime in the first century. Indications are, though, that when referrals in the New Testament are made to the scriptures, it is to this particular translation.

It seems that it is not until sometime around 140 that we see the first assembling of any texts that will be included in what we now call the New Testament. Referred to as *Marcion's Canon*, it listed ten letters attributed to Paul and a version of the Gospel of Luke. Following this, many others began to suggest their own possible canons, including such early Christian theologians as Irenaeus, Tertullian, Origen, Eusebius and Athanasius.

Just as with the Old Testament, there were many writings that may have been commonly circulated and accepted as true at the time that came to be considered pseudepigraphical and/or apocryphal through the New Testament canonization process. Some of these non-canonical texts may have included:

- Acts of Andrew
- Acts of John
- Acts of Paul
- Acts of Peter
- Acts of Peter and the Twelve
- Acts of Thomas
- Apocalypse of Peter
- Dialogue of the Savior
- Gospel of James
- Gospel of Mary
- Gospel of Peter
- Gospel of the Ebionites

- Gospel of the Egyptians
- Gospel of the Hebrews
- Gospel of the Nazoreans
- Gospel of the Savior
- Gospel of Thomas
- Infancy Gospel of Thomas
- Secret Book of James
- Secret Mark
- Preaching of Peter
- Traditions of Matthias
- Thomas the Contender

It appears that the *complete* closing of the canon for the Roman Catholic Church did not actually occur until 382 at the Council of Rome. It was led by Pope Damasus I who, the next year, commissioned the Latin Vulgate edition of the Bible led by Jerome. Another Latin version, the Gutenberg Bible, was the first book to be printed on the newly invented Gutenberg printing press in 1455. The Roman Catholic Church includes the Old Testament Apocrypha in its Bible, and the Greek Orthodox and Ethiopian Orthodox churches include apocryphal texts as well.

In 1522, Martin Luther, founder of the Protestant Reformation, translated the Bible into German. He placed the books of the Old Testament

Apocrypha between the two testaments. Sometimes later translations of the Bible included the books and sometimes they did not.

English translations of the Bible had already begun with the handwritten Wycliffe Bible in 1384. Many more English translations have ensued since the invention of the printing press. Some of them are:

- William Tyndale's New Testament in 1526
- Myles Coverdale's Bible in 1535
- Tyndale-Matthews Bible in 1537
- Great Bible in 1539
- Geneva Bible in 1560
- Bishops Bible in 1568
- King James Bible in 1611
- English Revised Version in 1885
- American Standard Version in 1901
- New American Standard Bible in 1971
- New International Version in 1973
- New King James Version in 1982
- English Standard Version in 2002

Looking at how our present-day Bible came into being can help us more easily discern why claiming its literalism, inerrancy and divine inspiration is so problematic, not to mention the assertion that our Bible is the *only* word of God. We would have to ask, at least two questions: "According to whom?" and "Which one?"

To continue to maintain such claims and assertions requires us to profess, at the least, that:

✓ *None* of the texts declared apocryphal should have been included

✓ *All* of the texts declared pseudepigraphical were not written by whom the authors claimed themselves to be

✓ *Only* the texts that made it into the Bible were the ones that were meant to be included

✓ That men were so divinely inspired and led by God that no errors were made in translating any of the texts by hand or by typesetting

✓ Nor did any translator change the meaning of any of the texts according to what he personally thought they really meant to say

The probability is that the Bible you read and study today is not only *not the only* word of God, but that there may be other words of God that you have been unwilling to take into consideration.

What if John 21:25, KJV, is one of the verses in the Bible that we should take quite *literally*?

And there are also many other things which Jesus did, the which, if they should be written every one, I suppose that even the world itself could not contain the books that should be written.

What if God has said more than what is in the Bible? What if he *still* has more to say?

Chapter Five

Is the Bible the *Final* Word of God?

If the Bible is the final word of God, then God has not said anything worth writing down as scriptural since its creation. Another way to ask the question might be, "Has God not had anything else important to say since the words in the Bible?" History indicates that nothing could be further from the truth.

Obviously God has indeed had a lot to say since the completion of the Bible. For instance, almost immediately following Jesus' crucifixion, his followers began to disagree about what God was telling them regarding the meaning of Jesus' life and death. Was the message just for Jews? Did it also include the Gentiles? If it did include the Gentiles, were they to become Jews first?

The letters in the New Testament attributed to Paul indicate that almost everyone in the churches was disagreeing with everyone else about almost everything, and even the churches were disagreeing with each other. It appears this was the main reason that most of the letters were written.

Twelve years after Constantine and Licinius issued the Edict of Milan in 313 granting religious tolerance in the Roman Empire, there was so much infighting going on in early Christianity that Constantine called for the Council of Nicaea in 325 to begin addressing some of the issues. As more and more issues surfaced, more and more councils had to be called. The issues they dealt with then are still controversial today. They include such questions as:

- Is Jesus the same as God or lesser than God or greater than God?

- Is the Holy Spirit the same as God or lesser than God or greater than God?

- Is the Holy Spirit the same as Jesus or lesser than Jesus or greater than Jesus?

- Is the Holy Spirit divine?

- Was Jesus divine or human or both or neither?

- Was Jesus born human and then became divine?

- Did God incarnate as Jesus or did he indwell and inspire Jesus?

- If Mary gave birth to Jesus and Jesus is God, is Mary the mother of God?

- Are we born sinful and in need of salvation as soon as we are born, or do we have free will and therefore can choose not to sin?

- If we are born sinful, how can God choose to punish us for something over which we have no control?

- If we have free will to choose not to be sinful, why can we then not be perfect?

There were also those arguments on what writings should be included in the New Testament, and those arguments still continue today. Of the twenty-seven books in the New Testament, thirteen (almost half) of these were attributed to the authorship of Paul, a man who never met Jesus during his lifetime and who based his sole authority as an apostle upon visions from God. One of these is especially interesting.

> *I knew a man in Christ above fourteen years ago, (whether in the body, I cannot tell; or whether out of the body, I cannot tell: God knoweth;) such an one caught up to the third heaven (2 Corinthians 12:2, KJV).*

Paul's most famous vision, of course, is the one he had on the road to Damascus which he interpreted as being a visit from Jesus himself.

Of the thirteen books finally attributed to Paul, scholars today still disagree on his authorship of six of them (again, almost half). The still disputed books are: Ephesians, Colossians, 2 Thessalonians, 1 & 2 Timothy and Titus.

One thing that doesn't seem to be quite as disputed today is that the gospels were written after the influence of Paul and were probably *not* written by the apostles Matthew, Mark, Luke and John. This may very well mean that the Bible does not include any first-hand accounts of the life of Jesus.

Another issue that doesn't seem to be quite as disputed today is that the Revelation of John was probably not written by the John who was a disciple of Jesus. The church councils experienced so much uncertainty over this matter that Revelations was the last New Testament book to be widely accepted as scripture.

What one church council would declare to be the final word of God on a matter would later be repudiated by a subsequent council. During these debates, many who were repudiated as heretics at the time are now recognized as being saints who were hearing the word of God. Many who were perceived as hearing the word of God at the time are now determined to have been heretics.

The first Christian martyrs may have been put to death for blasphemy against the one true God or for refusing to worship the Roman emperor and all the gods, but long after these persecutions ended, Christians were actually killing *each other* to declare the final word of God on a matter.

After the Protestant Reformation, groups who declared to know the final word of God grew even more numerous. This gave rise to the development of such religious groups as the Lutherans, Calvinists, Anglicans and Anabaptists. Of course, factions also arose within these about the final word of God and denominations began to expand exponentially. Just an abbreviated list might include:

American Methodist Episcopal

Apostolic

Assembly of God

Christian Church

Christian Science

Church of Christ

Church of God

Community

Congregational

Disciples of Christ

Episcopal

Free Will Baptist

Full Gospel

Jehovah's Witness

Mennonite

Missionary Baptist

Mormon

National Baptist

Nazarene

Pentecostal

Presbyterian

Primitive Baptist

Quaker (Society of Friends)

Scientology

Seventh Day Adventist

Southern Baptist
Unitarian
Unitarian Universalist
United Methodist
Unity

Chances are wherever you have gone to church in the past or wherever you might go to church in the future, there is always someone who will testify to knowing the final word of God on a matter and proposing that others do not.

What if God still has more to say?

Most Christians believe that God is alive and well and at work in the present-day world. If this is true, then why must his *final* word have been so long ago? What is someone really saying when they quip, "God said it. I believe it. That settles it."? Could they be closing their ears to what else God might still have to say?

The question we may really be asking at this point is, "Do you believe in the supremacy of God?"

If you do, then he cannot be limited in any way—not in *what* he chooses to say or to *whom* he chooses to say it or *when* he chooses to say or *where* he chooses to say or *how* he chooses to say it.

Otherwise, you are setting yourself up arrogantly to proclaim, as a mere mortal, that you personally know the very mind of God.

The keys to the car are not usually given to a young child because he is not mature enough to understand how to use them. Perhaps the keys to God's kingdom are not given to us all at once for the very same reason.

Truly I tell you, unless you change and become like children, you will never enter the kingdom of heaven (Matthew 18: 3, KJV).

When we were children, most of us knew we didn't already know everything. We were open to exploration and discovery and lifelong learning. Somewhere along the way, of course, we became rebellious teenagers who knew just about everything about everything! We hung out with the clique that validated our view of the world and we had very little to do with those outside our own chosen peer group. But hopefully as we matured, we realized we didn't have all the answers to all the questions and that we might not even know all the questions we should be asking. We became more open to the possibility that those outsiders just might have something to contribute to our lives as well.

Perhaps we can become like little children again and confess that we really and truly don't already know everything there is to know, especially about God. And maybe God doesn't try to tell us everything at once, just like we don't with our own children. Conceivably, the word of God could be so personal that he speaks to us at the *place* we are on our path in a way that we best can understand at the *time*.

This might even help explain why there are so many differences in the way Christians hear and interpret the word of God. God forbid, it might even help explain why there are so many differences among religions.

What if we could be open to the possibility that God will continue to speak and reveal himself to us if we'll leave behind the fundamentalism of religions *about* him and embrace the fundamentals of relationship *with* him?

Chapter Six

Resurrecting Relationship

In the *Introduction* to this book, I shared that there could be any number of reasons why someone would become a born-again Christian.

*It could have been a natural, normal process of growing up in your specific family. It could have been a particularly dark time in your life and the message of Jesus brought you light and hope. It could have been your life was in absolute shambles and you begged for God to intervene and give you direction. It could have been any number of other reasons as well, but in summary, **you probably wanted a direct, personal relationship with your creator.***

Each of our lives can attest to that fact that relationships can be a funny thing. The longer we're in one, the more we learn about the other person, and also ourselves. We usually begin a relationship believing we already know all we need to know about ourselves and even the other person, but many places along the way we're forced to grow and change in areas of which we had never dreamed.

Another thing about relationships is that the relationship you have today will not be the same relationship you have tomorrow, much less the same relationship you had at the beginning.

When I was baptized in my teenage years as a born-again Christian, I knew absolutely nothing about most of the matters I've been writing about in this book. I certainly had never heard anything about biblical literalism, inerrancy or divine inspiration. And I also wasn't the least bit familiar with

- the religious differences among Jesus' disciples after his crucifixion

- the discord within and among the early churches to whom the disciple Paul is said to have written

- the long and heated debates of the church councils

- the countless other texts that could have been included in our biblical canon

- the innumerable transcripts and translations of the texts that were included, or

- that there were a whole heck of a lot of other churches out there in other Christian denominations that didn't believe the way I was being taught to believe.

As I learned these things, my relationship with God changed. But my relationship with religion changed as well. I dared to look at what God may have said to others at different places and different times. I really wasn't that surprised that the five major religions—Hinduism, Buddhism, Judaism, Christianity and Islam—had such dissimilarities, but I was that they had so many similarities.

I found that from very ancient times there are similar stories about creation and a great flood and a god having a son with a mortal woman and then that son going through the cycle of birth, death and resurrection. All the religions had their own versions of the Golden Rule and philosophies about eternal life and the afterlife and how we should treat our fellow man in this life.

And then I discovered something that was incredibly inspirational, and then completely confounding. All of the religions seemed to be based upon a spiritual experience that someone had with the divine that led to their having an ongoing relationship with the divine. But once that encounter became a religious movement, *the religion would put limits on what the experience was and what the relationship could be.*

Limiting an unlimited God just didn't seem like good religion to me. Slowly but surely, my relationship *with* God became more important to me than any religion *about* God. My own personal experience of the divine became more powerful to me than any system of *belief* in someone else's experience, even if a religion was founded upon it.

My own personal relationship with God began with a Bible that I believed was the literal, inerrant, divinely inspired and final word of God. But with all healthy relationships, my relationship with God has grown and changed and developed as I have learned more—about myself and about God. And what I have learned has brought me into an even closer relationship with God.

If I had been born at a different place at a different time, my relationship with God probably would have begun with a different set of scriptures and their transcripts and translations and interpretations. It seems to me now that God does indeed speak to all of his children in a way that they can best understand at the time and place. Unfortunately, this doesn't mean that we always *completely* understand the words of God at the time and place any more than a child completely understands the words of a parent. This misunderstanding can happen no matter how hard the parent tries to talk on the child's level. So the parent, and God, has to keep trying to communicate in different ways.

I came to this conclusion about God speaking in different ways from a moral dilemma.

I've already shared that when I was much younger, it wasn't much of a stretch for me to believe that I personally was sinful and on my way to hell. I was just glad that God wanted to save me from it. As a matter of fact, I was so happy to accept Jesus Christ as my personal Lord and Savior that I did it twice!

My hesitation about hell came later. It began with being told why some other people would end up in hell. Some would be there because

1. they had never ever heard the gospel of my Lord and Savior, Jesus Christ, and/or

2. they were followers of another religion.

Life began to get complicated for me after that. First of all, if someone had never even heard the gospel of Jesus Christ, how could my loving and merciful God let them go to hell for something they didn't know? When I questioned the logic of this, I was just told that it was the responsibility of all Christians to make sure that everyone heard the gospel. The burden of that became unbearable—it would be *my* fault if they ended up in hell.

Second, it didn't seem fair to me that my God would allow someone to suffer in hell for following another religion. Now mind you, it wasn't because I considered that their religious beliefs could actually be valid. It was because I couldn't understand why God would penalize someone for following the teachings of their parents and the culture in which they lived. The cards were just stacked too high against them! Again, when I questioned this, I was told it was the responsibility of all Christians to make sure that followers of other religions were taught the error of their ways. Again I learned, it would be *my* fault if they ended up in hell.

I wish I could say the logic—or illogic—of it all was what finally broke down my belief in hell, but it was much more subjective than that. Even I, a mere mortal, couldn't justify these people going to hell for the reasons given. God, who I believed to be much more loving and compassionate and merciful than I, certainly wouldn't.

It had never crossed my mind at the time— believe it or not—*I didn't deserve to go to hell either!* It wasn't because I believed I was too good to go. I was more aware than anyone else of all my imperfections and shortcomings and failures—my dirty little sins and transgressions. But it dawned on me that I had never really said or done anything for which our own legal system would put me in jail for even a limited amount of time, much less for life. And if I did end up in jail temporarily or in prison for life, even we sinful human beings believed that inflicting pain and suffering on another human being was inhumane. It didn't seem possible to me that we were more humane than God. I was being taught, though, that hell wasn't just a short-term or long-term sentence; it was an *eternal* one.

It might be helpful at this point to explore from where our present-day concept of hell came. I don't believe you'll find it in the Bible.

You may find a Hebrew word *sheol* that is translated in a lot of ways: to ask or to demand or the grave or the place of the dead. Or there is a Greek word *gehenna* that supposedly describes a place where Ahaz, a king of Judah, sacrificed his own children in a fire. The Greek word *hades* is found, but it seems to mean pretty much the same thing as the Hebrew *sheol*. There's also another Greek word *tartaros* that seems to mean a prison or punishment.

Originally the concept of hell seemed to mean just a *place* where the dead go. Along the way it developed into a *bad place* where the dead go. And then it developed into a *bad place where bad people go*. It seems Lucifer, Satan and the Devil went though related transitions as well. In all likelihood, our present-day vision of the torment and torture of hell probably comes from Dante's *Inferno*, the first part of a three-part epic poem titled *The Divine Comedy* written in the early 1300s about a man's journey from darkness to light. You'll find all the hellfire and brimstone you can there, along with detailed descriptions of the most sadistic punishments of pain and suffering imaginable. It's not exactly the sort of place a parent would allow a child to go, even if they had been really bad.

Could it be that in our growing relationship with God that our belief in hell is one of the areas in which we need to be open to additional growth? As children, we may have tried to be good because we were afraid of our parents. Hopefully we've grown past that. But have you substituted that earlier fear of your parents with a present-day fear of God?

Could it be that in our growing relationship with God that our fear of him is another one of the areas in which we need to be open to additional growth? Most of us realize the implausibility of finding a healthy and meaningful relationship in a scenario where one of the parties is in fear of the other—for example, a wife afraid of her husband. So it begs us to ask a question. Is fear really a good basis upon which to have a relationship with God?

If you're desperately feeling the need to rush to the Bible to find passages to prove to me the existence of hell and the need to fear God, please relieve yourself of this burden.

First, I've already put forward how conflictual the Bible—and how it came to us—can be. Yes, I am well aware that 2 Timothy 3:16 states, "All scripture is given by inspiration of God, and is profitable for doctrine, for reproof, for correction, for instruction in righteousness" (KJV). But I've also already conveyed that the author of this book is highly disputed. Nonetheless, whoever he is, his reference to "scripture" at the time would have to have been to what Christians refer to as the *Old* Testament.

Second, my relationship with God is more important to me than a book believed by many to be divinely inspired because it says it is. If I state here that *this* book is divinely inspired, does it make it so?

Third, and most important to me personally, is that my relationship *with* God is more important to me than any religion *about* God, including yours. Your relationship with God may include your fearing him and believing in hell. Mine *presently* does not.

So, you might ask, why is the word "presently" in the last sentence in *italic*? Because my relationship with God today is not the same relationship I will have with God tomorrow, much less the same relationship I had with God at the beginning. He has not has his final word—or work—with me. And I get the feeling that his voice and actions will continue throughout eternity, whether anyone is listening or not.

I hope I will be listening.

Fundamen-talisman

74

Chapter Seven

Fundamen-talisman

If you'll remember at the beginning of this book, I wrote in the preface:

> *If you are a Christian fundamentalist and your beliefs are working for you because you know beyond a shadow of a doubt that they are right and real, this book is probably **not** for you. If you are a Christian fundamentalist and are beginning to question some of the beliefs you've been taught along the way, this book **may** be for you. If you are—or once were—a Christian fundamentalist and your beliefs just aren't working for you anymore, this book is **definitely** for you.*

It has been my intent from the very beginning of this book to resurrect the fundamentals of relationship with God from the fundamentalism of religion about God.

If your fundamentalist relationship with God is right and real for you, then I wasn't writing this book for you. You didn't have to read and you don't have to quarrel with it.

If your fundamentalist relationship with God was bringing up some questions in you, I hope this book has been helpful in looking at some of those possible questions. It may have brought up even more of them.

If your fundamentalist relationship with God just isn't working for you anymore, I hope this book will free you from trying to force God into a fundamentalist framework. I personally trust that following truth will set us free, and have faith that truth is truth no matter from whence it comes.

Remember when I discovered something that was incredibly inspirational, and then completely confounding? It was that all of the religions seemed to be based upon a spiritual experience that someone had with the divine that led to their having an ongoing relationship with the divine. But once that encounter became a religious movement, *the religion would put limits on what the experience was and what the relationship could be.*

As I said, limiting an unlimited God just didn't seem like good religion to me.

So now I feel no need to limit God or what my relationship with God can be.

I feel no need to limit what *your* relationship with God can be.

I feel no need to limit what God chooses to say to you or when God chooses to say it to you or where God chooses to say it to you or how God chooses to say it to you.

I feel no need to limit God to a specific sex or age or race or color or religion or denomination or belief system or creed or law or culture or national origin or political party.

I feel no need to limit God to just one set of religious scriptures or to having just one son. All scriptures could have truth, and God may have had lots of other sons and even daughters and wives.

I feel no need to limit my relationship with God to just one physical incarnation. God may give me multiple lifetimes to experience, expand and elevate. Perhaps the meaningful path of eternal life is not found in its sufferings and crucifixions and deaths, but rather in its joys and resurrections and transfigurations.

I feel no need to limit God to being outside of or apart from me. In our search for God, we all could be fish in a pond looking for a drink of water. Our day of judgment may not be so much a day of reckoning as it is a day of self-evaluation where we personally get to experience the ripples of the pebbles we've thrown into the pond of life. Have we added to, or subtracted from, the waves of love in the world? Compassion does not have to be compliance, nor does service have to be servitude.

I feel no need to limit my exposure to any new or different information or discoveries about the past or the present or the future. All truth only deepens my relationship with God, and I don't have to begin with my own version of the truth and accept only the evidence which supports it. The scientific method with its need for control variables and repeat performances isn't big enough to measure my relationship with God, nor is my religious education and present spiritual consciousness big enough to completely comprehend it.

I feel no need to limit my relationship with God to just my present questions and potential answers. Experience has taught me the more convinced someone is that they have answers, the less willing they are to hear any questions. I have found this to be true not only in religion, but in science and politics as well. If you're willing to accept without question any one area in your life, what else might you be willing to accept without question in other areas of your life?

I feel no need to limit God to this planet or solar system or galaxy or universe. If there are other species in addition to the human race, whatever truth I learn in relationship to them will only enlighten my relationship with God.

I feel no need to limit your relationship with God by trying to impress you with mine. I can share with you where I seem to be in my relationship presently, but if it's a healthy one, hopefully it will grow by leaps and bounds and I'll have something even more meaningful to share with you later on.

I feel no need to limit God in any way or my relationship with him or her or it or them.

As a result of my faith and trust in this unlimited relationship, everyone and everything can become sacred to me because of its potential part in the continual conversation I'm having in my growing relationship with God. This conversation and relationship can continue through the best of times and the worst of times, through times of ascension and through what appear to be apocalyptic times, because the real meaning of the word "apocalypse" is *to reveal what is hidden.*

In trying to describe something beyond description, I coined the word **fundamen-talisman** from the merging of the words *fundamental* and *talisman.* It's because my present relationship with God is *fundamentally mysterious and mystical.*

Fundamentally, the most mysterious and mystical revelation may end up being that my unlimited relationship with an unlimited God may also mean that I, too, am limitless. I'm even open to the possibility—yea, the probability—that my relationship with God will continue to grow even after my death.

So what do I believe? Well, right now. . . .

Epilogue

The Golden Rule

I shared with you in Chapter Six that I wasn't overly surprised to find so many dissimilarities among the religions, but I was pleasantly surprised to find that they had so many similarities. One of the parallels I discovered was regarding this passage of scripture we've come to know as *The Golden Rule*:

> *Therefore all things whatsoever ye would that men should do to you, do ye even so to them: for this is the law and the prophets (Matthew 7:12, KJV).*

I was delighted to come across a version of it in almost every religion on the planet. Each brought its own brand new, fresh perspective. Here are some of them for your own personal gratification and "instruction in righteousness."

❖ *Judaism*: What is hurtful to yourself, do not to your fellow man.

❖ *Islam*: No one of you is a believer until he loves for his brother what he loves for himself.

❖ *Hinduism*: Do not to others, which, if done to thee, would cause thee pain.

❖ *Buddhism*: In five ways should a clansman minister to his friends and familiars--by generosity, courtesy and benevolence; by treating them as he treats himself; and by being as good as his word.

❖ *Native American*: Do not condemn your brother until you have walked a mile in his moccasins.

❖ *Paganism*: May I do to others as I would they should do unto me.

But my mostest favoritest of all has to be a Yoruba proverb which says it all:

One who is going to take a pointed stick to pinch a baby bird should first try it on himself to feel how it hurts!

As you continue to resurrect the fundamentals of relationship from the fundamentalism of religion, I hope for you that you will be able to fly freely without someone pinching you with a pointed stick!

About the Author

Duann Kier is a spiritual intuitive or psychic whose life path has carried her from Christian fundamentalism to the belief that spiritual revelations are ongoing and can be received by all.

Trusting that the teacher will come when the student is ready, Duann actively engages individuals in the process of finding and following their own spiritual path. She is known for her high energy and sense of humor, and has over 25 years experience in training and development.

While serving as Organizational Development Specialist at Coastal Carolina Community College in Jacksonville, North Carolina, Duann was selected as Educator of the Year. She created the Personal and Professional Development Center in Morganton, North Carolina as well as the Career Consultation Center at Middle Tennessee State University in Murfreesboro. She also served as Program Director for the YWCA of Middle Tennessee in Nashville where her programs won multiple state and national awards.

She obtained the Master of Religious Education degree from New Orleans Baptist Theological Seminary and is an ordained minister. She has worked for a Southern Baptist college, church and newspaper as well as for the Southern Baptist Convention.

Fondly known as *The Skeptical Psychic* because she continuously examines her intuitive gift, Duann offers private and confidential spiritual or psychic readings known as Seer Sessions. She also performs weddings and other sacraments.

To join Duann's mailing list, go to her website at <u>www.DuannKier.com</u>.

Personal Notes:

Personal Notes:

Personal Notes:

Personal Notes:

Personal Notes:

Personal Notes:

Personal Notes:

Personal Notes:

Personal Notes:

Personal Notes:

Personal Notes:

Personal Notes:

Personal Notes:

Personal Notes:

Personal Notes:

Personal Notes:

Personal Notes: